Cambridge Discovery Education™

▶ **INTERACTIVE READERS**

Series editor: Bob Hastings

RESCUED
THE CHILEAN MINING ACCIDENT

B1+

Diane Naughton

CAMBRIDGE
UNIVERSITY PRESS

DISCOVERY
EDUCATION™

CAMBRIDGE UNIVERSITY PRESS
Cambridge, New York, Melbourne, Madrid, Cape Town,
Singapore, São Paulo, Delhi, Mexico City

Cambridge University Press
32 Avenue of the Americas, New York, NY 10013-2473, USA

www.cambridge.org
Information on this title: www.cambridge.org/9781107655195

First published 2014

Printed in Hong Kong, China, by Golden Cup Printing Company Limited

A catalog record for this publication is available from the British Library.

Library of Congress Cataloging-in-Publication Data

Naughton, Diane.
    Rescued : the Chilean mining accident / Diane Naughton.
        pages cm. -- (Cambridge discovery interactive readers)
    ISBN 978-1-107-65519-5 (pbk. : alk. paper)
    1. San José Mine Accident, Chile, 2010--Juvenile literature. 2. Mine accidents--Chile--Copiapó
Region--Juvenile literature. I. Title.

TN311.N38 2013
363.11'962234220983145--dc23

                            2013023920

ISBN 978-1-107-65519-5

Additional resources for this publication at www.cambridge.org

Layout services, art direction, book design, and photo research: Q2ABillSMITH GROUP
Editorial services: Hyphen S.A.
Audio production: CityVox, New York
Video production: Q2ABillSMITH GROUP

Contents

Before You Read:
Get Ready!

In 2010, the eyes of the world were on Chile. After a terrible accident, 33 men spent many days underground with no way out. Could they be saved?

Words to Know

Look at the pictures. Then complete the definitions below with the correct words.

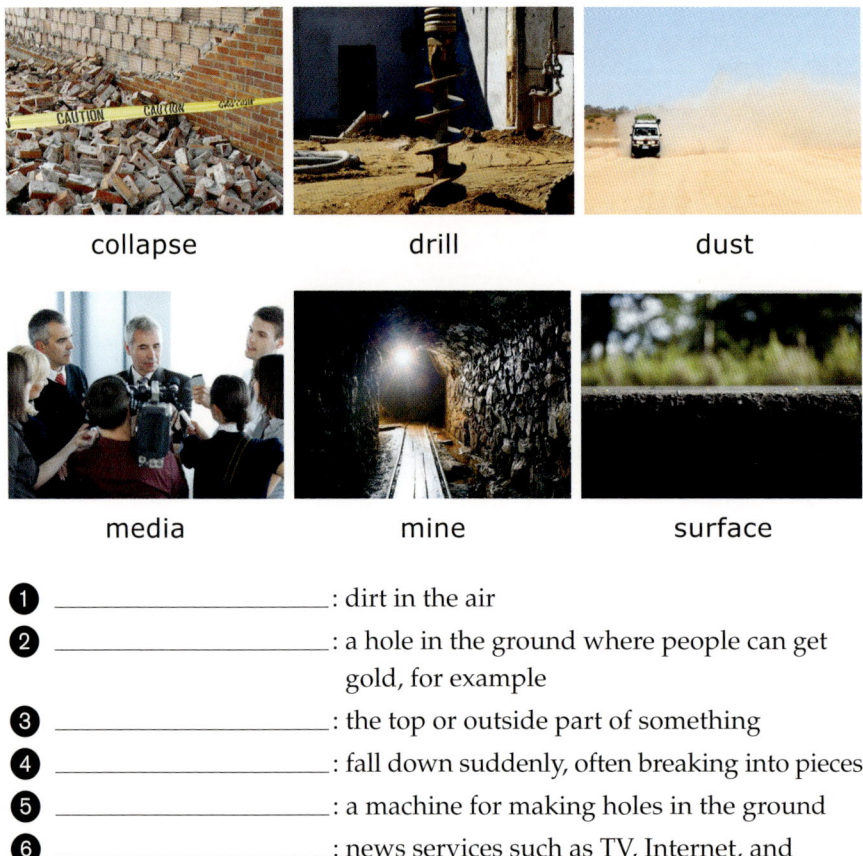

collapse   drill   dust

media   mine   surface

1. _____ : dirt in the air
2. _____ : a hole in the ground where people can get gold, for example
3. _____ : the top or outside part of something
4. _____ : fall down suddenly, often breaking into pieces
5. _____ : a machine for making holes in the ground
6. _____ : news services such as TV, Internet, and newspapers

Words to Know

Read the paragraph. Then use the highlighted words to complete the sentences below.

There are many mines all over the world, and they are often dangerous places to work. Disasters can happen especially if safety rules are not followed. Sometimes the walls or roofs of tunnels can collapse, and the miners get trapped because there is no way to escape. Normally in the mine there are special areas called refuges where miners can go in an emergency. In the refuge they will find things that they need to survive, like food and water. Sometimes, they have to stay there for a long time until the rescuers find them. For both the miners and their families, this experience can be terrible – a living nightmare that they will remember forever.

1 If someone is _____, they can't get out or escape from a place.

2 If you _____, you continue living after a terrible accident or illness.

3 _____ can happen suddenly and hurt or kill a lot of people.

4 A _____ is a frightening dream or something very bad that happens to you.

5 _____ are places where you are protected from danger.

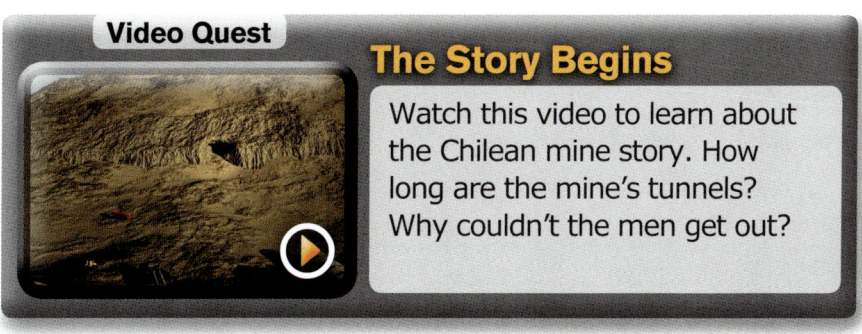

Video Quest

The Story Begins

Watch this video to learn about the Chilean mine story. How long are the mine's tunnels? Why couldn't the men get out?

CHAPTER 1

The Story Begins

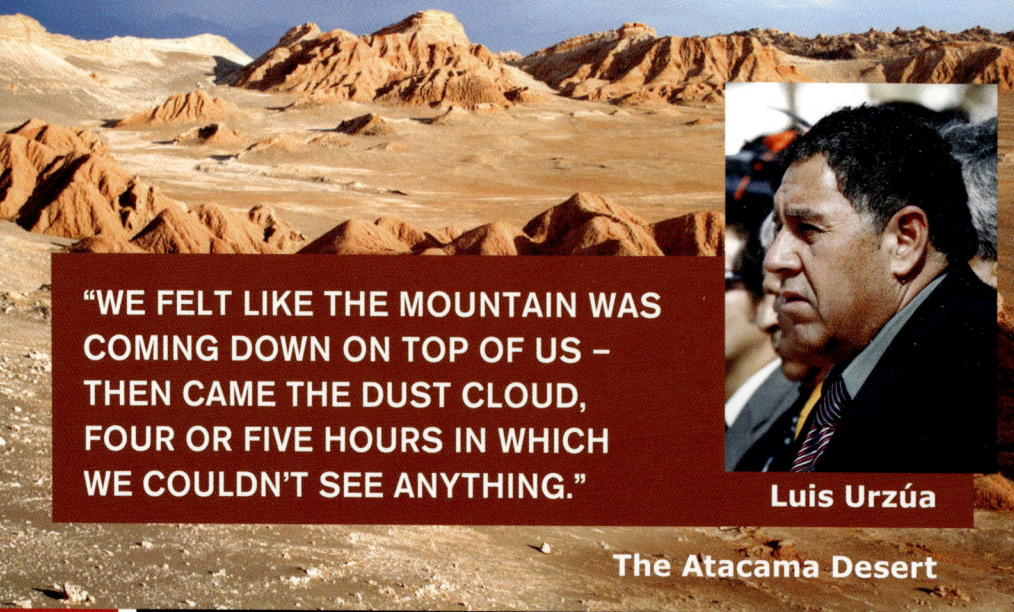

"WE FELT LIKE THE MOUNTAIN WAS COMING DOWN ON TOP OF US – THEN CAME THE DUST CLOUD, FOUR OR FIVE HOURS IN WHICH WE COULDN'T SEE ANYTHING."

Luis Urzúa

The Atacama Desert

With these words, the leader of a group of miners, Luis Urzúa, describes the terrible moment when the mine collapsed. It was 2 p.m. on August 5, 2010. Luis and 32 other men were working in the mine as usual. Suddenly rocks began to fall from the roofs and walls, making a cloud of **dust**. The nightmare that every miner has always imagined was coming true.

The confused, frightened men called out to each other in the dark. Who was dead and who was alive? Soon all 33 of them had been counted. Incredibly, all the miners had **survived**.

But what should they do next? The miners looked for a way out, but found none. They wondered if rescuers would come and how long it would take them. They asked themselves how they would **cope** while they waited. And so began a nightmare that those men will never forget.

The story started at the San José copper and gold mine in the Atacama Desert, in Chile, but reached the homes and the hearts of people all over the world. Copper mines have been very important in Chile for centuries, and most of them are in the Atacama Desert. This is one of the driest and most difficult places to live on Earth, but it is very important for the Chilean economy.[1] Chile gets about a third of its money by selling copper from these mines to other countries. So for many people, Chile is a country of mines, and the miners who work there are the heart of Chile.

....
[1] **economy:** the way a country makes and uses money

Copper pipes

Mining has always been a dangerous job, and accidents happen quite often all over the world. Some of these **disasters** have been really terrible. In France in 1906, an accident killed 1,099 miners, and in China in 1942, another accident killed 1,549 miners. Since then, however, better safety rules have made mines less dangerous places to work. In Chile, the safety in large mines was generally good in 2010, but in smaller mines, the rules were not always followed.

The San José mine was a small mine about 45 kilometers north of the town of Copiapó. It was also an old mine; it opened 121 years before the accident happened. Many people knew that the mine was unsafe. Between 1998 and 2010, there had been several accidents and at least three miners had lost their lives.

Courrières mine disaster, France 1906

The owners, the San Esteban Mining Company, had been fined[2] 42 times between 2004 and 2010 for not following safety rules. Workers were also paid more than in other mines to encourage them to work there. One leader of a workers' organization said that the managers worked "without listening to the voice of the workers when they say there is danger." Disaster was waiting to happen!

In the refuge

On the day of the accident, two groups of miners were working in the mine. When it collapsed, the group nearest the exit escaped. Urzúa and his group didn't. They were **trapped** 700 meters below the ground and five kilometers from the exit. The men managed to get to an emergency refuge where they found some food and water. But there was no daylight and it was very hot and dusty. And although they didn't know it yet, this would be their home for the next 69 days!

....

[2]**fine:** punish someone by making him or her pay some money

?

ANALYZE

How do you think the miners coped in the refuge? What **psychological** problems would they probably have?

CHAPTER 2

Above and Below the Ground

ABOVE THE GROUND, EXPERTS START PLANNING THE RESCUE, WHILE UNDER THE ATACAMA, THE MINERS START LEARNING TO SURVIVE.

Below the ground, Luis Urzúa immediately realized that things were very serious for the miners. As group leader, he started organizing the men. They went into different tunnels to look for a way out. But they found only rocks. Another possibility was to climb up through the ventilation[3] tunnel. It hadn't collapsed in the accident, but when the miners looked, they found there were no ladders. Although the company had been told during earlier safety checks to put ladders there, they hadn't done it. The men were definitely trapped.

[3]**ventilation:** a way of letting air in and out of a place

In modern mines, there are usually elevators that go from the **surface** to the tunnels in the mine below. However, the San José mine was very old and there were no elevators. The paths to the deeper parts of the mine were long and winding.[4] Because of this, Urzúa knew that a rescue operation would be very complicated. Maybe they would have to survive underground for many days. The miners would have to cope with many problems if this happened.

To get light, the miners could use the machines in the mine to charge[5] the batteries in their head lamps. They could also get a little natural water from the ground, but not enough. There was some water in the machines too, but it wasn't very clean.

Food was one of their biggest worries. There were only enough cans of food in the refuge for two to four days, so they had to make them last for as long as possible. Each miner was allowed a tiny piece of tuna fish, a spoonful of fruit, and some milk from those cans every 48 hours. It wasn't much. Two weeks after the accident, each miner had lost about eight kilos. Things were looking very bad!

[4]**winding:** not straight, for a road, river, or path
[5]**charge:** put electricity into something

On the surface, things were happening. Immediately after the accident, rescuers began looking for ways to get into the mine. Again and again, however, they had to stop their rescue plans when they reached a wall of rock. Heavy machines were used to try to break through the rock, but it was difficult.

On August 7, another part of the mine collapsed. Now, the rescuers were afraid to continue. They didn't know exactly where the miners were. If they continued, more rocks might fall and kill the miners. Fire captain Rafael González Pérez said, "Rocks, dust, darkness, heat – it is impossible." Breaking through to the miners in this way was no longer a possible solution.

Friends and relatives had begun arriving at the mine as soon as they heard news of the disaster. They wanted to see their loved ones safely above ground. Ten of them offered to go into the mine instead of the rescue team, but they weren't allowed. The rest of the Chilean people were following the progress of the rescue in the **media**, too. Many were unhappy about how little the government had done during a terrible earthquake[6] six months earlier. Now it was time for the politicians to do a better job. The whole country was with the miners. The government had to act.

President Sebastián Piñera returned quickly from a trip and started managing a complicated rescue plan. Three international teams of experts came to the mine and started drilling long, narrow holes in the ground. By doing this, they hoped to find out where the miners were. But it was a difficult job. The rock was very hard, and maps of the mine were so old that they were no longer right.

About two weeks after the rescue operation had begun, one of the drills broke through into an open space. The rescue teams thought the miners might be there, but there were no signs of life. Great sadness was felt across Chile and across the rest of the world, where many people were following the story in the news. It was almost impossible to believe that the miners could survive underground for this long. The rescuers began to lose hope. Families and friends began to think they would never see their loved ones again.

....

[6]**earthquake:** when the earth moves and buildings often collapse

President Piñera shows the miners' message to the world.

But the rescue plans continued, and on August 22, another drill broke into the mine. This time, when it was pulled back out of the ground, it was carrying a short handwritten message. It read, "WE ARE WELL IN THE REFUGE, ALL 33." There were shouts of joy[7] from the people waiting on the surface of the mine, and when President Piñera showed the message to the media, there were shouts of joy across Chile and all over the world, too.

A few hours later, video cameras were sent down the hole, and the world saw an amazing sight. The miners were very thin and dirty. They all had beards and none of them was wearing a shirt. But most important of all, 17 days after the accident, they were alive!

Now the rescuers had to think about two things: how to get the miners out and how to help them survive underground while they planned the rescue.

[7]**joy:** a strong feeling of happiness

First, they began sending food and medicine down the hole. Then they allowed relatives and friends to send letters. The rescuers warned the miners' loved ones, however, not to write about sad things. They were worried about the miners' psychological health. Bad news might make them depressed.

At first, the rescuers were afraid to tell the miners how long the rescue operation could take. But then, on August 25, they told them the truth. They might not be free until Christmas. The miners took the news surprisingly well.

The miners sent letters to their families, too, and on August 27, they made a 40-minute video of themselves. They also sang the national anthem[8] of Chile over a kind of telephone that was sent down the hole. They seemed to be coping well.

[8]**national anthem:** the song of a country

ANALYZE

Experts from NASA (the American space organization) were asked to help. Why do you think this was? How could a space organization help miners?

CHAPTER 3

Camp Hope

CLOWNS DANCING AND GIVING OUT CANDY, WOMEN DOING THEIR HAIR AND GETTING READY TO SEE THEIR MEN – A FESTIVAL? NO, JUST CAMP HOPE ON THE MORNING OF THE RESCUE!

After the accident, the miners' families slept in their cars near the mine for the first few nights. Then they started to put up tents and bring other useful things from home. The camp started to grow as more friends and relatives arrived. Some people lived there all the time. Others came from far away to visit at weekends. The rescuers also lived there, and the number of reporters grew and grew.

Tent homes at Camp Hope

Children playing at
Camp Hope

Women keeping warm
at Camp Hope

The government began to help to make the camp more comfortable. They built a kitchen, a cafeteria, and toilets. They started a regular bus service between Copiapó and the camp. Later they built a school and a children's play area. Workers from the city sent free hot meals, and about 70 police officers were brought by the government to help with safety at the camp. It was becoming like a small town. They even chose a leader, María Segovia, the sister of one of the trapped miners. She was good at organizing and speaking clearly. They called her *La Alcaldesa* (Mayor[9]).

It was very hot during the day and freezing cold at night. Life was hard, but people helped each other and new friendships grew. There were few quiet moments. Musicians performed on a small stage, and parties and games were organized for the children.

---

[9]**mayor:** the leader of a town or city

The flags

But, of course, nobody ever forgot for a minute why they were there. On a hill there were 32 Chilean flags and one Bolivian flag: a flag for each of their much loved miners. There were photos, too, and statues of saints.[10] And the people prayed and hoped that God would bring their men safely back home.

Under the ground, the men were also well organized. Each day, they spent eight hours working, looking after the refuge, and moving rocks that fell into the refuge because of the drilling. Urzúa made maps of the area around the refuge to help with the rescue, and another man kept a diary. The miner Yonni Barrios became the doctor of the group, and Mario Gómez became the religious leader.

Obviously, the men also had a lot of free time, so they wrote letters, played games, and exercised. One man, Edison Peña, became famous for running 10 kilometers a day in the mine tunnels.

[10]**saint:** in some religions, a dead person who helps the living and speaks for them to God

His wife, Angélica, managed to send some running shoes down to him in the refuge from Camp Hope. Another miner, Franklin Lobos, had once been a professional soccer player. While trapped in the mine, he received signed soccer shirts from teams all over the world.

Communication between the refuge and Camp Hope helped to keep hope alive. Miner Esteban Rojas had been married by law for 25 years, but he hadn't been married in church. His wife, Jessica, had always wanted a church wedding. It was at Camp Hope that she read a message from Esteban: "When I get out, let's buy the dress and we'll get married." Maybe one of the most romantic marriage proposals[11] ever!

But maybe not all the women were as happy with their men as Jessica. Marta had been married to Yonni Barrios for 28 years. When she met Susana Valenzuela at Camp Hope, they began to talk and she found out a terrible secret. Susana was waiting for Yonni to be rescued, too. They were lovers!

[11] **proposal:** the act of asking someone to marry you

Video Quest

Visiting Camp Hope

Watch this video to learn about Camp Hope. What does Elisabeth Segovia's husband change?

Phoenix

AT LAST THE BIG DAY ARRIVES: THE PEOPLE AT CAMP HOPE ARE EXCITED BUT FRIGHTENED, HOPEFUL BUT NERVOUS. WILL ALL GO WELL?

Earlier than expected, the rescuers finished drilling a tunnel that went from the surface to the miners' refuge. They put pieces of metal around the inside of the tunnel to make it stronger. The plan was to pull the miners up the tunnel in a metal capsule. This capsule was given the name "Phoenix" after a mythical[12] bird that died in a fire, but was reborn.

The capsule was only 54 centimeters wide, a little more than an average man's shoulders. It had to be narrow so that it didn't hit the sides of the tunnel. All the miners had lost weight, so they would be able to get inside. But there would be very little space. And they would be in the capsule for a long time.

Inside the capsule there were lights and a video connection. This meant that the miners could talk to the rescue workers as they traveled up to the surface.

[12]**mythical:** something that comes from a traditional story

The roof of the capsule was very hard, to protect the miner inside against falling rocks. There was enough air for about 90 minutes. At the bottom, there was an escape door. If the capsule stopped moving, the miner would have to climb down the tunnel to get back to the refuge.

On October 12, shortly after 11 p.m., Manuel González, a rescuer working on the surface, traveled down to the refuge in the capsule. It took him 18 minutes to reach the miners. The rest of the rescue team and waiting relatives were singing the Chilean national anthem. Now it was time to start bringing the miners up.

The order in which the miners would be brought out had already been decided. The first four miners had to be in good health and have a lot of experience working in mines. This was so that they could communicate calmly with the rescuers or escape successfully if something went wrong. Number 5 would be the least healthy. And the strongest miner still in the refuge would leave last. This was because they knew that it would be psychologically very hard to be the last person left alone underground. The rescuers thought it might take as long as 33 hours to bring all the miners up to the surface.

Manuel González arrives in the mine.

Before the trip in the capsule, each miner was given dark sunglasses to wear. The light of day would hurt their eyes after 69 days of being in the dark.

Florencio Ávalos was number one. He entered the capsule, they closed the door, and rescuers started bringing him to the surface. At 12:11 a.m. on October 13, he got out of the capsule smiling. He hugged his crying wife and seven-year-old son, and then he hugged President Piñera. Millions of people all over the world watched on television and wanted to hug him, too.

Hardly anyone in Chile slept that night. Instead, people watched as the miners, one by one, were brought up from the mine. Surprisingly, many of the miners were full of energy despite their experience.

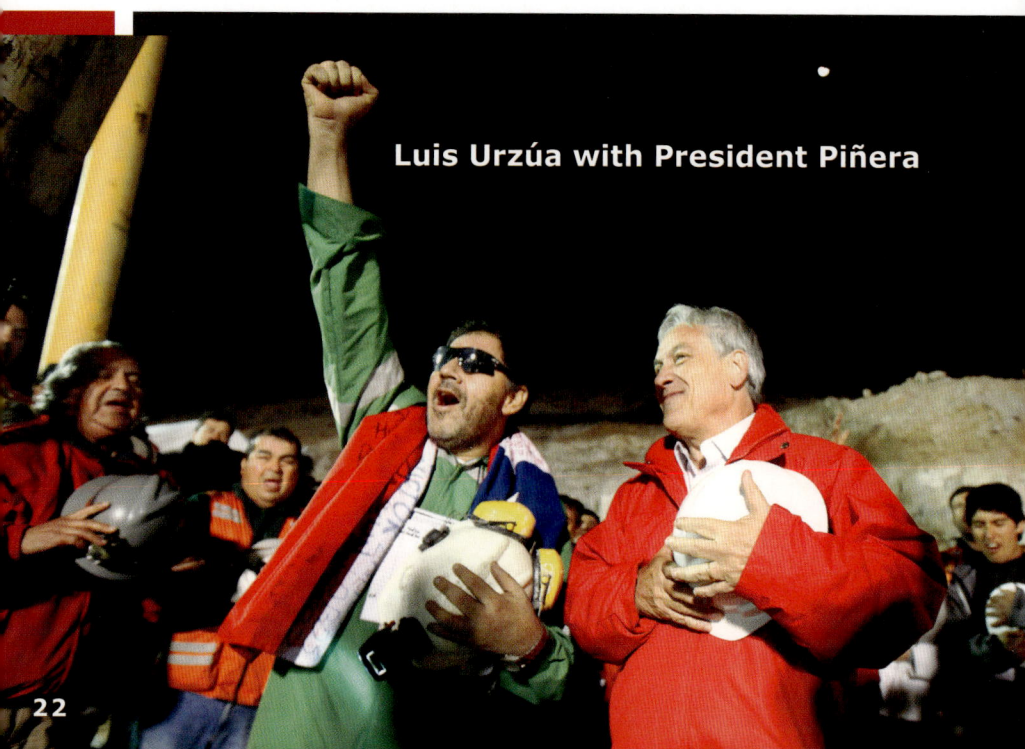

Luis Urzúa with President Piñera

They jumped and shouted with joy, they kissed and hugged their loved ones. Franklin Lobos was given a soccer ball, and he kicked it around a bit. Smiling, he said, "This was the hardest match of my life."

Finally, miner number 33, Luis Urzúa, came out. He hugged his son and said to the president, "I give you this group of workers as I agreed I would." The president

Franklin Lobos with his soccer ball

replied, "I happily receive the group because you completed your duty,[13] leaving last like a good captain."

[13] **duty:** something you must do because it is part of your job or because it is right

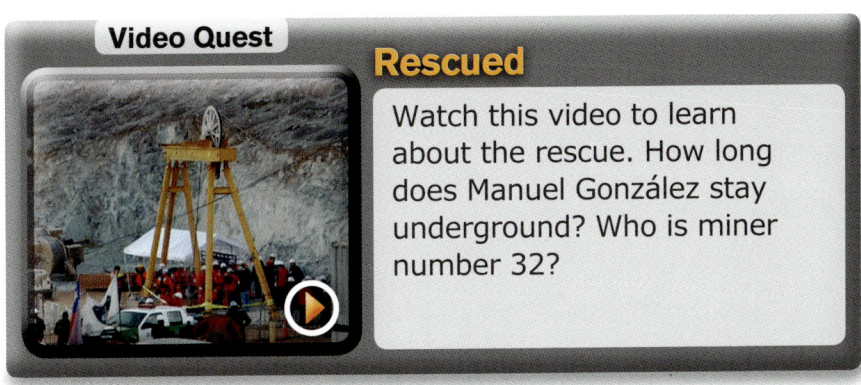

Video Quest

Rescued

Watch this video to learn about the rescue. How long does Manuel González stay underground? Who is miner number 32?

CHAPTER 5

What Do You Think?

THE MINERS ARE FREE, AND THEY ARE INTERNATIONAL HEROES. BUT WHAT WILL HAPPEN NEXT? WILL THEIR FUTURE STORY BE ONE OF HAPPINESS AND SUCCESS?

When the miners were pulled out of their dark prison, they were famous. People all over the world were interested in their story. And so was the media. After the rescue, the miners were taken to a hospital so that doctors could check their health. TV and newspaper reporters camped outside the hospital. When the miners were well enough to go home, the media went with them.

On October 17, a religious ceremony was organized at Camp Hope, and six miners and their families were there. The reporters were there too, and they were almost fighting with each other to get interviews.

The two-year-old granddaughter of one miner, Omar Reygadas, was pushed and she began to cry. Reygadas told the reporters, "I've had nightmares these days – but the worst nightmare is all of you."

Was it right to allow the media so near the miners during these difficult days? Was it necessary to protect the miners from reporters?

One year later, things were very different. The media had lost interest, and the miners were trying to get back to their lives. But it wasn't easy. Many had psychological problems, and it was hard to find work. The government gave them money, but very little. A few miners got well-paid jobs in mines, but most of them were unemployed or had low-paid jobs.

But one thing is certain. They could all be proud of themselves, their families, and the rescue workers. At a time of little hope, they worked bravely as a team and helped each other survive. They stayed strong and believed in life. And as a result, they survived.

A religious ceremony at Camp Hope

After You Read

Read the sentences and choose Ⓐ, Ⓑ, or Ⓒ.

1 Copper mining _____.

Ⓐ is extremely important in Chile

Ⓑ isn't important any more

Ⓒ began a hundred years ago in Chile

2 The San Esteban Mining Company had to pay some money to the government because their mine was _____.

Ⓐ foreign

Ⓑ quite old

Ⓒ dangerous

3 The miners made the emergency food last for _____.

Ⓐ about two days

ⓑ about fourteen days

Ⓒ more than a month

4 Some of the friends and relatives of the miners wanted to _____.

Ⓐ meet the President

Ⓑ try to enter the mine

Ⓒ help with the drilling

5 While underground, one of the miners surprised the world by _____.

Ⓐ learning a language

Ⓑ writing a long book

Ⓒ doing a lot of exercise

6 The capsule was called Phoenix because of _____.

Ⓐ a mining tradition

Ⓑ a Chilean rescuer

Ⓒ an animal from stories

7 The first four miners to leave the refuge were _____ .

- (A) the strongest
- (B) the weakest
- (C) very ill

8 Miner Omar Reygadas said that his worst nightmare was _____ .

- (a) the mine
- (b) the media
- (c) his health

Complete the Text

Complete the text with the correct words from the box.

capsule	collapsed	drills	miners	refuge	rescuers	survive

JOY AT CAMP HOPE – THE MINERS COME HOME!

There were tears of joy at Camp Hope today as the last of the 33 **1** _____ stepped out of the rescue **2** _____ into the light of day. The men had spent 69 days in a **3** _____ 700 meters below the ground after part of the mine **4** _____ . They had managed to **5** _____ for 17 days on very little food and water taken from the ground and the mine's machines. The **6** _____ were beginning to lose any hope of finding them when, on August 22, they found a message on one of their **7** _____ . It said, "We are well in the refuge." The miners were alive!

?

EVALUATE

A miner's job is very dangerous. Do you think miners should earn more money than top athletes or highly educated people like doctors?

Answer Key

Words to Know, page 4
1 dust **2** mine **3** surface **4** collapse **5** drill **6** media

Words to Know, page 5
1 trapped **2** survive **3** Disasters **4** nightmare
5 Refuges

Video Quest, page 5
The mine's tunnels are 160 kilometers long. There was a big rock in the mine's exit.

Analyze, page 9   *Answers will vary.*

Analyze, page 15   *Answers will vary.*

Video Quest, page 19
Her husband changes their new baby's name to *Esperanza*, which means "Hope" in English.

Video Quest, page 23
González stays under the ground for 25 hours and 14 minutes. Miner number 32 is Elizabeth Segovia's husband, Ariel.

Choose the Correct Answers, page 26
1 A **2** C **3** B **4** B **5** C **6** C **7** A **8** B

Complete the Text, page 27
1 miners **2** capsule **3** refuge **4** collapsed **5** survive
6 rescuers **7** drills

Evaluate, page 27   *Answers will vary.*